KU-132-474

The Life of

Helen Keller

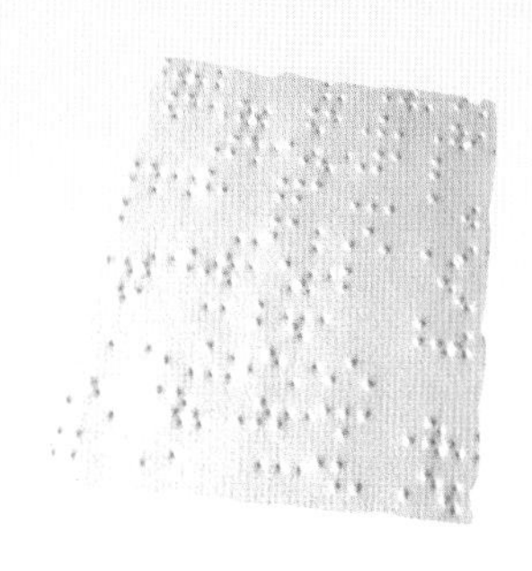

Emma Lynch

Heinemann
LIBRARY

First published in Great Britain by Heinemann Library, Halley Court, Jordan Hill, Oxford OX2 8EJ, part of Harcourt Education.
Heinemann is a registered trademark of Harcourt Education Ltd.

Editorial: Lucy Thunder and Harriet Milles
Design: Richard Parker and
Tinstar Design Ltd (www.tinstar.co.uk)
Picture Research: Melissa Allison and Fiona Orbell
Production: Camilla Smith

Originated by Repro Multi-Warna
Printed and bound in China by
South China Printing Company
The paper used to print this book comes from sustainable resources.

ISBN 0 431 18096 2
09 08 07 06 05
10 9 8 7 6 5 4 3 2 1

British Library Cataloguing in Publication Data
Emma Lynch
Helen Keller. – (The Life of)
362.4'1'092
A full catalogue record for this book is available from the British Library.

Acknowledgements
The Publishers would like to thank the following for permission to reproduce photographs:
pp. **4**, **14**, **18**, **19** Corbis/Bettmann; pp. **5**, **6**, **10**, **12**, **13**, **17**, **20**, **21**, **23**, **24** American Foundation for the Blind; p. **7**, **8/9**, **15** Judith Lawton/Harcourt Education Ltd.; p. **11** Science Photo Library/Library of Congress; p. **16** Ronald Grant Archive; p. **25** Science Photo Library; p. **27** The Callahan Museum of the American Printing House for the Blind

Cover photograph of Helen Keller, reproduced with permission of Getty Images/Hulton Archive. Page icons: Judith Lawton/Harcourt Education Ltd.

The Publishers would like to thank Rebecca Vickers for her assistance in the preparation of this book.

Contents

Words shown in the text in bold, **like this**, are explained in the Glossary.

Who was Helen Keller?

Helen Keller had a childhood illness that left her unable to see or hear. She had to learn to live as a **deaf** and **blind** person.

Being deaf and blind made Helen's young life very hard.

Helen then spent her life helping other deaf-blind people. She worked hard for a better life and treatment for them. Her work helped many people.

Helen helped us to understand more about deaf and blind people.

Childhood illness

Helen Keller was born on 27 June 1880. Her family lived in Tuscumbia, Alabama in the United States of America. When Helen was born, she could see and hear.

Helen's parents were Kate Adams Keller and Captain Arthur Keller.

Helen's illness may have been **meningitis**.

Helen became very ill in February 1882. She was only 19 months old. Helen got better, but she was now **deaf** and **blind**. She would never learn to talk.

Growing up wild

As Helen grew up, she was wild and hard to live with. She could not see, hear, or speak. She did not understand the world around her.

Helen was angry. She could not talk to other people, or understand them. Her relatives thought she should be put in an **asylum**. Her mother said no.

Helen would scream and smash things.

Alexander Graham Bell

When Helen was six years old, her parents went to see a special doctor. He told them that Helen would never see or hear again.

Helen's parents wanted to make her life better.

The doctor told the family to speak to Alexander Graham Bell. He was famous because he had **invented** the telephone. Now he wanted to help **deaf** children.

Bell knew about deaf people because his mother and wife were deaf.

A teacher for Helen

Alexander Graham Bell helped the Kellers to find a teacher for Helen. She was called Anne Mansfield Sullivan. Anne had once been nearly **blind** herself.

Anne Mansfield Sullivan became Helen's teacher.

Anne had had **operations** to help her see. She still could not see very well. It was hard for her to find work. In March 1887, Anne Sullivan became Helen's teacher.

Anne came to live with Helen and her family at this house in Tuscumbia, Alabama.

A new friendship

Anne taught Helen how to spell words with her fingers. She gave Helen a doll and wrote 'd-o-l-l' with her finger into Helen's hand. Then she tried 'c-a-k-e'.

Helen learned to spell words, but she did not understand them.

Anne also tried to make Helen behave better. After a while, Helen became less wild. She stopped having temper tantrums.

Helen and Anne became close friends.

A miracle!

On 5 April 1887, Anne put Helen's hand in water. She spelled 'w-a-t-e-r' on to Helen's other hand. Suddenly Helen understood. The cool running liquid had a name – it was called water!

This picture is from a film called *The Miracle Worker*. It shows the moment that the **miracle** happened.

Now Helen wanted to know the words for everything she touched.

Helen wanted Anne to teach her more and more words. Within a few hours, she knew 30 words!

So much to learn

Anne taught Helen how to read **Braille**. This is a special writing for **blind** people. You read Braille with your fingers, by feeling raised dots on the page.

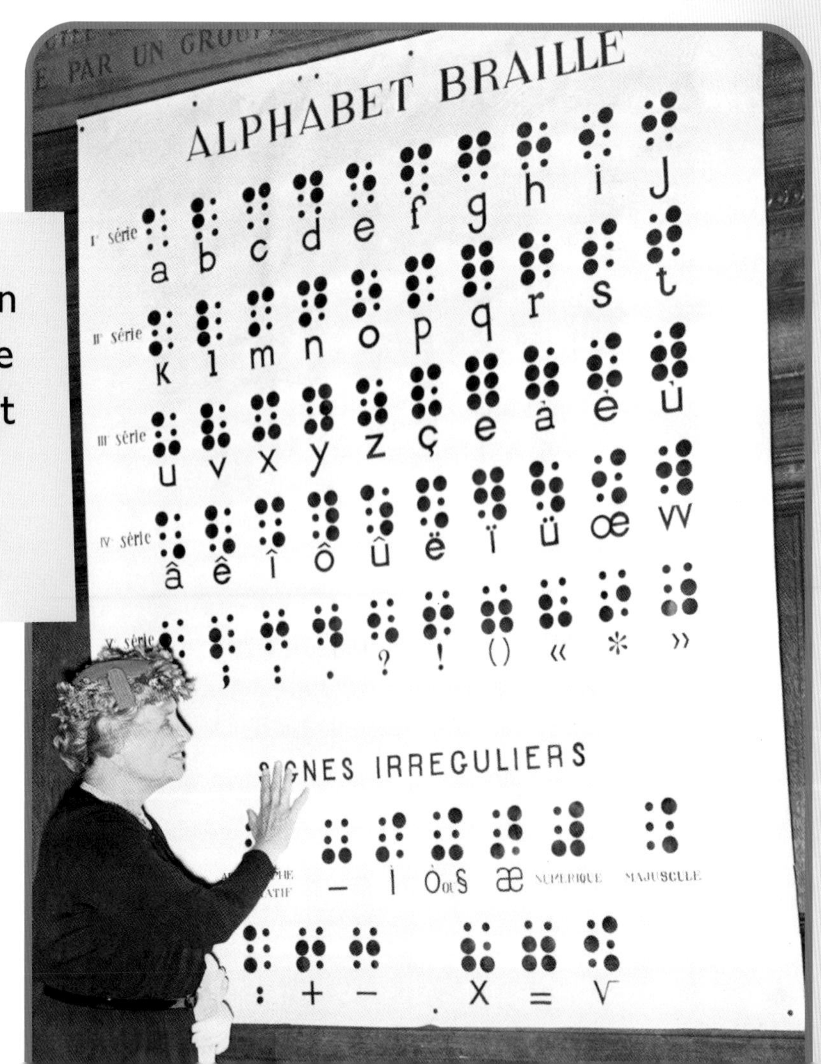

This is Helen when she was older. She is standing in front of the Braille alphabet.

Helen learned more than anyone thought would be possible. She was the first **deaf-blind** person to get a university **degree**. Helen and Anne became famous.

Helen was given her degree on 28 June 1904.

Touring the world

Helen and Anne went on **lecture** tours. They spoke to people about Helen's life. Helen answered people's questions. Anne **translated** every sentence.

Helen spent the next 50 years on lecture tours! This is a brochure from one of her lectures.

The First Appearance on the Lecture Platform of

HELEN KELLER

And her Teacher Mrs. Macy (Anne M. Sullivan)

SUBJECT

"The Heart and the Hand," or the Right Use of our Senses

Under the exclusive Management of
J. B. POND LYCEUM BUREAU
Metropolitan Life Building
New York City

Helen gave lectures all over the world.

In 1918, Helen began to work for **charities**. She wanted to make life better for **blind** people. At that time blind people had little education and often lived in **asylums**.

A long and busy life

Anne Sullivan died on 20 October 1936. Helen still worked all around the world. She became ill in 1961 and stopped her tours and **lectures**.

Helen was still writing and reading when she was 80 years old.

In 1964, US President Lyndon Johnson gave Helen a special medal for her work. Helen Keller died on 1 June 1968 when she was 87 years old.

Helen was given The Presidential Medal of Freedom for her work with **deaf-blind** people.

Why is Helen famous?

Helen Keller helped us to understand about the needs of **deaf** and **blind** people. She showed the world that deaf-blind people can do great things.

Helen told US President John F Kennedy about her work.

Today, there are machines that would have changed Helen's young life. Helen Keller's work helped to bring about the **invention** of these machines.

This **Braille** machine helps blind people to read the writing on a computer screen.

More about Helen

We can find out more about Helen Keller from the American Foundation for the **Blind**. There are photos of Helen and **artefacts** from her life and **lecture** tours.

Helen wrote a book about her life in 1902.

There are websites and books about Helen's life. There is even a film about Helen and Anne, called *The Miracle Worker*. Helen's childhood home is now a **museum**.

This special plaque was made for Helen in 1907. Helen liked it so much that she wrote her name on it.

Fact file

- The Royal National Institute for the **Blind** (RNIB) helps people who are blind or have sight problems in the UK.
- Louis Braille (1809-1852) invented **Braille** writing. He lost his own sight when he was young. He spent his life helping blind people.
- Helen Keller Day is celebrated in the United States on 27 June every year.
- All her life, Helen wanted to talk. When she was a teenager, she went to the Wright-Humason School for the **Deaf**. She learned how to make a few sounds. Only the people close to her could understand them.

Timeline

1880 Helen Keller is born on 27 June

1882 Helen Keller loses her sight and hearing

1886 The Kellers meet Alexander Graham Bell

1887 Anne Sullivan becomes Helen's teacher on 3 March

1887 On 5 April, Helen begins to understand that everything has a name

1900 Helen goes to Radcliffe College

1902 Helen writes The Story of My Life

1913 Helen and Anne start their **lecture** tours

1936 Anne dies on 20 October

1955 Helen publishes a book called Teacher about Anne Sullivan

1961 Helen stops her lectures and tours

1968 Helen dies on 1 June

Glossary

artefact something from long ago that we can still look at today

asylum hospital for people who were blind, deaf or mentally ill

blind not able to see

Braille special writing for blind people, made up of raised dots that are read by touch

charity organization that helps people in need

deaf not able to hear

degree award you are given when you pass exams at university

disability something that takes away a person's power or strength and makes it harder for them to do things

invent to think of and make something for the first time

lecture someone talking about something they know about; an audience comes to listen

meningitis very serious illness that affects the brain

miracle something amazing that no-one could have believed might happen

museum where pieces of art or parts of history are kept

operation work that a doctor does in hospital to make a part of the body get better

translate explain so that someone can understand

Find out more

Books

Real People: Helen Keller, Pamela Walker, (Welcome Books Children's Press, 2001)

An older reader can help you with this book:

The Story of My Life (100th Anniversary Edition), Helen Keller (Signet Classics, 2002)

Websites

http://www.rnib.org.uk/xpedio/groups/public/documents/code/InternetHome.hcsp
Information about the Royal National Institute for the Blind and the work it does for blind people.

http://www.helenkellerbirthplace.org/
Information about Ivy Green museum at Helen Keller's birthplace.

Places to visit

You can visit Helen Keller's grave at:
Washington National Cathedral, Massachusetts and Wisconsin Aves NW, Washington, DC, USA
001 (202) 537-6207

Index

Titles in *The Life of* series include:

Hardback 0 431 18110 1

Hardback 0 431 18102 0

Hardback 0 431 18096 2

Hardback 0 431 18095 4

Hardback 0 431 18093 8

Hardback 0 431 18104 7

Hardback 0 431 18103 9

Hardback 0 431 18094 6

Hardback 0 431 18097 0

Find out about the other titles in the Heinemann Library on our website www.heinemann.co.uk/library